BOOK ANALYSIS

Written by Jean-Bosco d'Otreppe
Translated by Rebecca Neal

The Fall

BY ALBERT CAMUS

ALBERT CAMUS

FRENCH WRITER, PLAYWRIGHT, ESSAYIST
AND PHILOSOPHER

- **Born in Mondovi (Algeria) in 1913**
- **Died in Villeblevin in 1960**
- **Notable works:**
  - *The Stranger* (1942), novel
  - *The Myth of Sisyphus* (1942), essay
  - *The Plague* (1947), novel

The Algerian-born French author Albert Camus (1913-1960) is a Nobel Laureate and one of the major writers of the 20th century. A deeply committed intellectual, philosopher, journalist, playwright and novelist, his reflections on the absurd, which he expressed in a nuanced, sensitive and humane way, proved very influential during his time.

Widely admired but sometimes criticised, Camus made a considerable impact across the world with his novels *The Plague* (1947) and especially *The Stranger* (1942). He met an untimely death following a car accident in 1960.

THE FALL

GUILT IN THE WORLD OF THE ABSURD

- **Genre:** novel
- **Reference edition:** Camus, A. (1957) *The Fall*. Trans. O'Brien, J. New York: Knopf.
- **First edition:** 1956
- **Themes:** guilt, selfishness, duplicity, human nature, decline

First published in 1956, *The Fall* is the third and final part of the trilogy which began with *The Stranger* and *The Plague*.

The Fall is the confession of Jean-Baptiste Clamence, a French former lawyer who has gone to seek refuge in the mists of Amsterdam. In a long monologue, the narrator recounts his life in Paris, which was filled with glory, conquests and fine speeches, until the day he was crossing a bridge in the dead of night and failed to help a drowning woman. This was the start of a wake-up call for him, and as a result of this he cannot help but condemn the old life that he loved so much, made up, like all lives in his time, of selfishness, cowardice and vanity.

SUMMARY

The Fall comprises six chapters corresponding with five days (each chapter covers one day, apart from chapters 4 and 5). The first three chapters are set before the account of the drowning, while the final two recount what happened afterwards. This structure allows the separation between life before and after the tragedy to be marked more clearly, by emphasising the changes in the protagonist's mental state.

BEFORE THE TRAGEDY

Camus suddenly plunges the reader into the hazy, smoky atmosphere of 'Mexico City', a bar tucked away in the heart of Amsterdam, where Jean-Baptiste Clamence is starting a conversation with a compatriot whose name we never learn. Throughout the narrative, he is the only person who speaks; his compatriot is only there to listen to his confession.

Jean-Baptiste has left Paris, where he was a cultured lawyer, to become a judge-penitent in Holland under the pseudonym Clamence. His profession allows him to live comfortably while completely accepting his duplicity. It involves publicly despising himself and accusing himself of all manner of evils, but in doing so the portrait that he offers to his contemporaries "becomes a mirror" (p. 140), which allows him to freely judge them in turn. Since one "couldn't condemn others without immediately judging oneself, one had to overwhelm oneself to have the right to judge others", he explains (p. 138).

Clamence describes to his listener the "dream" that Holland represents and his love for the Dutch. These people always look absent, with their heads in "that fog compounded of neon, gin and mint emanating from the shop signs above them" (p. 13). The discussion ends in the cold of the night by a bridge which, following a resolution that he made, Clamence does not want to cross.

The next day, the judge-penitent talks about his life in Paris. He led the existence of an esteemed man, constantly defending widows and orphans to quench his thirst for charity. Handsome and admirable, and aware of his many virtues, he only looked for the highest points. However, one evening as he was admiring the Seine from the Pont des Arts, a laugh burst out of nowhere behind him. Clamence returned home feeling troubled, and then noticed in his bathroom mirror that he had a double smile.

Clamence admits that his life has not been the same since this episode. The harmony which previously characterised his life seems to be insidiously breaking apart. He gradually becomes aware of the futility of his existence and realises that he was driven to do good by a thirst for domination and power rather than by a thirst for virtue. The judge-penitent leaves his interlocutor to go talk to the manager of the Mexico City, worried by the theft of a painting.

On the third day, as he reconsiders his life, he reveals his shame and remembers another story, which he also recounts to his listener. One night, as he was returning home, he heard the body of a young woman he had just passed fall into the water. Surprised, he admits that he did not move: "I was trembling, I believe, from cold and shock. I told myself that I had to be quick and I felt an irresistible weakness steal over me. I have forgotten what I thought then. 'Too late, too far...', or something of the sort." He then says that he continued to listen without moving, before leaving without telling anyone (p. 70).

AFTER THE TRAGEDY

On the fourth day, Clamence and his companion visit the island of Marken, with its dead, flat, colourless landscapes. Over the course of the conversation he confesses to his friend that, contrary to what he might think, he is not perfect and even has some enemies. He is not surprised by this because, according to him, people judge in order to avoid being judged. But this discovery has revealed to him another part of himself, namely his intrinsic duplicity: "Then I realised, as a result of delving in my memory, that modesty helped me to shine, humility to conquer, and virtue to oppress. I used to wage war by peaceful means and eventually used to achieve, through disinterested means, everything that I desired" (pp. 85-86).

Aware of his faults and furious that his contemporaries continue to consider him perfect, he chose to make his duplicity public. Making himself appear ridiculous, he disturbed public opinion through unpleasant remarks, both in his defence speeches and during social events. He also decided to throw himself wholeheartedly into debauchery, and this new way of life granted him some relief. Debauchery is freeing because it does not create any obligations.

However, one day he was by the side of the ocean when a black mark caught his eye and reminded him of the shape of a drowning person. He understood then that he would never be able to forget his guilt: "I had to submit and admit my guilt. I had to live in the little-ease" (p. 109). He explains that all men must recognise their faults because this is their destiny. Indeed, the real reason for Christ's agony "is that *he* knew he was not altogether innocent" (p. 112).

Clamence, who is now unwell, welcomes his interlocutor into his bedroom and confesses that he once condemned his cellmate in a prison camp to death by drinking his water. He judged that, because of his responsibilities, his own survival was more important than that of his companion.

He also shows him the famous Van Eyck (Flemish painter, c.1390-1441) painting *The Just Judges*, which was stolen years earlier and sold in the Mexico City. Clamence persuaded the manager of the bar to give it to him. Now, with "Justice being definitively separated from innocence – the latter on the cross and the former in the cupboard" (p. 130), he can finally become a judge-penitent.

> "Perhaps the rest would be taken care of subsequently; I would be decapitated, for instance, and I'd have no more fear of death; I'd be saved. Above the gathered crowd, you would hold up my still warm head, so that they could recognize themselves in it and I could again dominate – an exemplar. All would be consummated; I should have brought to a close, unseen and unknown, my career as a false prophet crying in the wilderness and refusing to come forth" (pp. 146-147).

But his interlocutor is only a Parisian lawyer.

CHARACTER STUDY

JEAN-BAPTISTE CLAMENCE

He is a former lawyer who, disappointed with his life in Paris, has come to Amsterdam under a false name (Jean-Baptiste Clamence is a pseudonym and we never learn his true identity) to carry out his new profession as a judge-penitent.

It must be noted that, as a former lawyer, Clamence is a highly skilled speaker. He is the one who coolly conducts his confession and structures his narrative, piquing his listener's interest as he wishes.

However, this rhetoric ultimately reveals an ambiguous and paradoxical figure, torn between lies and the truth: "You, for instance, *mon cher compatriote*, stop and think of what your sign would be. You are silent? Well, you'll tell me later on. I know mine in any case: a double face, a charming Janus, and above it the motto of the house: 'In any case, don't rely on it.' On my cards: 'Jean-Baptiste Clamence, play actor.'" (p. 47) Janus is a Roman god with two faces. Clamence admits that he lies to others just as he lies to himself. He recognises that a lie can say as much as, if not more than, the truth: "Sometimes it is easier to see clearly into the liar than into the man who tells the truth. Truth, like light, blinds. Falsehood, on the contrary, is a beautiful twilight that enhances every object" (pp. 119-120). However, through his confession he seeks to move towards the truth. This is the paradox of this character.

The question, then, concerns the meaning of his confession. We could stop at his explicit wish to practice his new profession as a judge-penitent. And yet, it is also possible to discern a genuine cry for help in the former lawyer's monologue. His distress is perceptible behind the ever-present irony of his narrative, but also in his illness, when his interlocutor visits him in bed at home as he is at his lowest ebb:

> "Don't bear down too hard on me. I'm like that old beggar who wouldn't let go of my hand one day on a café terrace: 'Oh, sir,' he said, 'it's not just that I'm no good, but you lose track of the light.' Yes, we have lost track of the light, the mornings, the holy innocence of those who forgive themselves." (p. 145).

THE INTERLOCUTOR

The man whom Clamence is addressing teaches us a lot about the judge-penitent. He is a Parisian lawyer who is also travelling to Amsterdam. As such, many elements allow the reader to see in the interlocutor a second Clamence who, taken in by the judge-penitent's rhetoric, gradually becomes aware of his duplicity and loses his innocence as he realises his own guilt. Furthermore, the structure of the narrative, which condemns him to silence, also expresses and underlines his status as a victim.

The interlocutor is consequently condemned to be a victim who is nonetheless guilty of his misdeeds. Clamence, on the other hand, must constantly find new victims so as to continue to be a judge-penitent. He has therefore trapped himself in a sadomasochistic hell.

While he claims to accuse himself in order to accuse others, it seems to us that his method results in him degrading himself through the reflection of himself that he discovers in others.

The fact that Camus did not choose a police officer as his interlocutor, but rather a Parisian lawyer who resembles Clamence's clone, indicates his desire to show that the judge-penitent cannot escape his condition. Clamence is not a happy man; he is someone who is trapped by his own guilt. In other people, all he does is observe and admire the spectacle of his own degradation. He does not try to find new hope or a chance at redemption.

ANALYSIS

GUILT

The theme of guilt is central to *The Fall*. The difficulty for Clamence, unlike, for example, Meursault in *The Stranger*, is that nobody comes to condemn him. No court comes to relieve him of his wrongdoing. He is therefore his only judge, and as a result remains a slave to his own crimes. To avoid this, he hopes that one day the painting will be found, but no police officers find their way to his house to discover *The Just Judges*.

Consequently, Clamence's indictment of himself obliges us to see in ourselves the faults which unconsciously gnaw at our minds, and shows us that degradation is an innate part of our nature. We are all guilty.

WORDS THAT ENSLAVE

Clamence shapes his narrative in accordance with his own will. His words serve to imprison. In his monologue, the interlocutor is denied a part and has no voice at any point in the chapter. Of course, Clamence pretends to listen to him, but really he only takes from his listener the things that suit him to create a monologue that is deaf to the other man's words. As a result, Clamence shuts others away in his speech and denies their individuality and specific features in order to classify them as he wants to. "With me" explains Clamence, "there is no giving of absolution or blessing. Everything is simply totted up, and then: 'It comes to so much. You are an evil-doer, a satyr, a congenital liar, a homosexual, an artist, etc.' Just like that. Just as flatly" (p. 131). A person who is judged in this way has no right to defend themselves; the judge-penitent makes whatever he wants of their personality and condemns them to be whatever he says.

In this way, afraid of his own freedom (a man who presents himself as free is responsible for all his actions and all his choices, which has a frightening side), Clamence enslaves his interlocutors and, through his speech, imprisons them in the logic of his thoughts: "In philosophy as in politics, I am for any theory that refuses to grant man innocence and for any practice that treats him as guilty. You see in me, *très cher*, an enlightened advocate of slavery" (pp. 131-132).

AMSTERDAM

The Fall is the only one of Camus's works that is set far away from the Mediterranean sunlight that the author was so partial to. The choice of the Dutch city is however understandable, since the atmosphere there very closely resembles Clamence's state of mind.

In Amsterdam, a city of rain, fog and cold, Clamence finds the very things that drove him to not save the woman who had fallen in the Seine. In the heart of Amsterdam, he is once again a prisoner of the things that led him to his misdeed. He therefore seems to choose this city in order to accept his crime, to wallow in it and dwell in it.

Amsterdam is also a city where nothing is clear. Shaped by

the twists and turns of its canals, it has a dark side and, in the halftone of its colours, a lie can no longer be distinguished from the truth. No blinding light passes through the city. Clamence, who, as we have already shown, observes lies in order to understand the truth, feels at home in this capital, where he can take refuge in the myths that reside there, in dreams and in paintings.

However, Clamence also likes to find the light, bright morning colours. He cannot stop thinking about Greece, where everything is brightness and light. In short, it seems that he hopes one day to find grace and return to living in the light. But is his hope real? The irony of the last lines of the books seem to suggest that it is not:

> "You yourself utter the words that for years have never ceased echoing through my nights and that I shall at last say through your mouth: 'O young woman, throw yourself into the water again so that I may a second time have the chance of saving both of us!' A second time, eh, what a risky suggestion! Just suppose, *cher maître*, that we should be taken literally? We'd have to go through with it. Brr ...! The water's so cold! But let's not worry! It's too late now. It will always be too late. Fortunately!" (p. 147).

THE PLACE OF *THE FALL* IN CAMUS'S PHILOSOPHY

Camus is known for having developed the notion of the absurd. For him, the absurd is a feeling that man experiences in the course of his existence. This feeling results from the confrontation between man, who asks himself many questions about his life, and the unreasonable silence of the world, which remains deaf to his appeals. Man must subsequently recognise and face up to the absurdity of his existence. Camus believes that it is useless to trust in a hypothetical God or to envisage oneself in an uncertain future. Instead, we must live on our certainties alone, make the most of the present and have faith in man. This is the only way to find happiness.

In its way, *The Fall* is a novel which tells the reader about this feeling of the absurd. Clamence follows the same progression as Meursault in *The Stranger*. He starts off by living without asking himself too many questions, but, insidiously and over time, a collection of elements (the laughter on the bridge, the body falling into the Seine, etc.) pull him out of his apathy and cause him to progressively re-evaluate his life. Like Meursault, he then realises the futility of his existence but, unlike the protagonist of *The Stranger*, he does not at all show man's revolt in the face of the absurdity of his condition. Indeed, Clamence no longer believes in mankind and despairs of humanity, whereas Meursault, illustrating Camus's precepts, lives fully in the present and in doing so recovers his life and his freedom.

It seems that when Camus wrote *The Fall*, three years before his death, he wanted to become more critical towards the moral code he had espoused earlier in his life. In any case, he abandons any idealism, and illustrates the fog and the lifeless atmosphere that our humanity so often finds itself in.

FURTHER REFLECTION

SOME QUESTIONS TO THINK ABOUT

- After reading this book, how can we envisage human justice?
- Clamence believes that divine justice, if it were to exist, is less terrifying than the justice of men. Explain.
- After reading this book, do you think that we still have the right to be happy, or should we first of all recognise our own guilt?
- In your opinion, why doesn't Clamence report himself to the police directly for stealing the painting?
- Why, in your opinion, does Clamence show the gloomy, desolate landscape of the island of Marken to his interlocutor, admit that he enjoys looking at it and at the same time often hopes to see the clear morning light descending over Amsterdam?
- In what way is the absurd present in this work?
- Why, in your opinion, does Clamence use so much humour and irony?
- In what way does *The Fall* respond to *The Stranger*?

We want to hear from you!
Leave a comment on your online library
and share your favourite books on social media!

FURTHER READING

REFERENCE EDITION

- Camus, A. (1957) *The Fall*. Trans. O'Brien, J. New York: Knopf.

MORE FROM BRIGHTSUMMARIES.COM

- Reading guide – *The First Man* by Albert Camus
- Reading guide – *The Just Assassins* by Albert Camus
- Reading guide – *The Myth of Sisyphus* by Albert Camus
- Reading guide – *The Plague* by Albert Camus
- Reading guide – *The Stranger* by Albert Camus

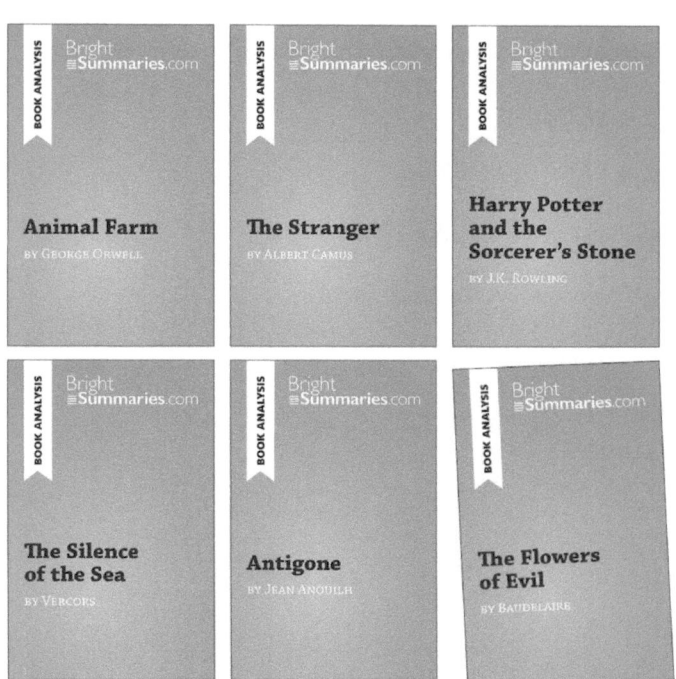

© **BrightSummaries.com, 2016. All rights reserved.**

www.brightsummaries.com

Ebook EAN: 9782806281005

Paperback EAN: 9782806287557

Legal Deposit: D/2016/12603/646

Cover: © Primento

Digital conception by Primento, the digital partner of publishers.